PRESIDENTS' DAY

LYNN HAMILTON

www.av2books.com

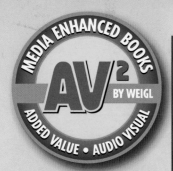

AV² by Weigl brings you media enhanced books that support active learning.

AV² provides enriched content that supplements and complements this book. Weigl's AV² books strive to create inspired learning and engage young minds for a total learning experience.

Go to **www.av2books.com**, and enter this book's unique code. You will have access to video, audio, web links, quizzes, a slide show, and activities.

BOOK CODE

K 5 0 4 1 4 4

Audio
Listen to sections of the book read aloud.

Video
Watch informative video clips.

Web Link
Find research sites and play interactive games.

Try This!
Complete activities and hands-on experiments.

Due to the dynamic nature of the Internet, some of the URLs and activities provided as part of AV² by Weigl may have changed or ceased to exist. AV² by Weigl accepts no responsibility for any such changes. All media enhanced books are regularly monitored to update addresses and sites in a timely manner. Contact AV² by Weigl at 1-866-649-3445 or av2books@weigl.com with any questions, comments, or feedback.

Published by AV² by Weigl
350 5th Avenue, 59th Floor
New York, NY 10118
Website: www.av2books.com   www.weigl.com

Library of Congress Cataloging-in-Publication Data

Hamilton, Lynn, 1964-
 Presidents' Day / Lynn Hamilton.
    p. cm. -- (American celebrations)
 Originally published: c2004.
 Includes index.
 ISBN 978-1-60596-773-8 (hardcover : alk. paper) -- ISBN 978-1-60596-931-2 (softcover : alk. paper) -- ISBN 978-1-60596-938-1 (e-book)
 1. Presidents' Day--Juvenile literature. 2. Washington, George, 1732-1799--Juvenile literature. 3. Lincoln, Abraham, 1809-1865--Juvenile literature. 4. Presidents--United States--History--Juvenile literature. I. Title.
 E176.8.H36 2011
 394.261--dc22
                        2009050991

Printed in the United States of America in North Mankato, Minnesota
1 2 3 4 5 6 7 8 9 0 14 13 12 11 10

052010
WEP264000

Editor Heather C. Hudak   **Design** Terry Paulhus

Every reasonable effort has been made to trace ownership and to obtain permission to reprint copyright material. The publishers would be pleased to have any errors or omissions brought to their attention so that they may be corrected in subsequent printings.

Weigl acknowledges Getty Images as its primary image supplier for this title.

CONTENTS

What is Presidents' Day?

Presidents' Day is celebrated on the third Monday in February. On this **patriotic** holiday, U.S. citizens show their appreciation for presidents of the United States. It is a day to honor the presidents and the roles they have played in the growth and success of the United States.

George Washington was the first president to be honored with a national holiday on his birthday. Abraham Lincoln was remembered with public ceremonies after his death. Citizens of the United States greatly valued the leadership of both presidents. People still admire and appreciate their achievements today. Many Presidents' Day events honor one, or both, of these presidents. Communities pay tribute to other presidents, too.

Special Events
THROUGHOUT THE YEAR

JANUARY 1
NEW YEAR'S DAY

 FEBRUARY (THIRD MONDAY)
PRESIDENTS' DAY

MARCH 17
ST. PATRICK'S DAY

SUNDAY IN MARCH OR APRIL
EASTER

MAY (LAST MONDAY)
MEMORIAL DAY

JUNE 14
FLAG DAY

JULY 4
INDEPENDENCE DAY

AUGUST (FIRST SUNDAY)
FAMILY DAY

SEPTEMBER (FIRST MONDAY)
LABOR DAY

OCTOBER (SECOND MONDAY)
COLUMBUS DAY

NOVEMBER 11
VETERANS DAY

DECEMBER 25
CHRISTMAS DAY

Presidents' Day History

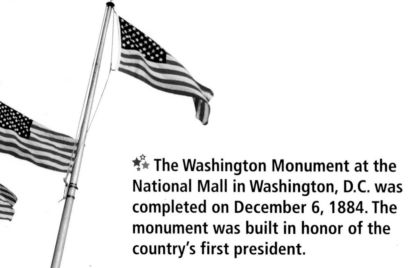

For more than 200 years, people have celebrated George Washington's birthday. An annual Birthnight **Ball** honored President Washington near his home in Alexandria, Virginia. The ball was based on the British tradition of throwing a ball on the **monarch**'s birthday.

Washington's Birthday became a national holiday in 1885. In 1932, festivities were held throughout the year to mark the 200th anniversary of his birth. Many citizens planted trees in his honor.

The Washington Monument at the National Mall in Washington, D.C. was completed on December 6, 1884. The monument was built in honor of the country's first president.

Presidents John Adams and Thomas Jefferson both died on July 4, 1826. This is the anniversary of the signing of the Declaration of Independence.

Congress passed a law in 1968 that changed the dates of several holidays. The celebration of Washington's birthday was moved to the third Monday in February. This gave Americans a long weekend. President Richard Nixon renamed the holiday Presidents' Day. He believed all U.S. presidents should be honored. Congress did not approve this change. The holiday is still officially named Washington's Birthday. However, in many states, the holiday is known as Presidents' Day.

Past and Present Celebrations

WASHINGTON'S ANNUAL Birthnight Ball was held at Gladsby's Ballrooom in Alexandria. Today, people still celebrate Washington's Birthday with a ball at Gladsby's.

ORIGINALLY, PRESIDENTS' Day was celebrated with large balls and receptions. Today, many people have family gatherings or visit important places in presidential history, such as Mount Rushmore. Some towns hold reenactments of Presidents' Day parties, such as the Birthnight Ball.

IN 1885, President Chester Arthur made Washington's Birthday a national holiday. In 1968, President Nixon moved Presidents' Day to the third Monday of February.

Important People

George Washington was born on February 22, 1732. He grew up to become a skilled military leader. Many **colonists** lived in the eastern United States. They wanted to become an independent nation. To stop their efforts, Great Britain declared war on the U.S. This war was called the **American Revolution**. Washington guided troops during the war.

After the American Revolution, Washington led the creation of the United States Constitution. In 1789, Washington was voted the first president of the United States. He is often called the "Father of the Country."

Abraham Lincoln was born in Kentucky on February 12, 1809. He served on the Illinois state government as a young man. He also practiced law. Lincoln was elected to Congress in 1847. After serving his term, he stayed active in law and politics and fought against **slavery**.

★★ As a young man, George Washington led soldiers in defending the United States against attacks from the French.

In 1861, Lincoln became the 16th president of the United States. He served as president during the **Civil War**. In 1863, Abraham Lincoln issued the **Emancipation Proclamation**, bringing an end to slavery. Lincoln was killed days after the Civil War ended. On April 14, 1865, Lincoln attended a play at Ford's Theater. During the play, an actor named John Wilkes Booth shot him. The next day, Lincoln died. Crowds gathered at train stations to pay their respects.

The year after Abraham Lincoln died, memorial ceremonies were held to honor him. His birthday was made a state holiday in Illinois in 1892. In 1959, on the 150th anniversary of his birth, ceremonies took place throughout the year.

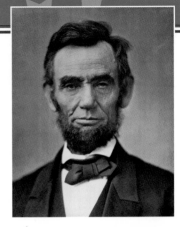

Abraham Lincoln had little formal education. However, he was an excellent speaker. His powerful speeches gained him respect.

First-hand Account

"The last was a brilliant one; 'twas on the General's birth night. Never did I see such a collection of handsome ladies. I do not believe that Versailles [the Royal French Court] or Saint James's [the Royal British Court] ever displayed so much beauty. I wish you had been present."

In 1783, John Marshall, a future Chief Justice of the United States Supreme Court, attended a Birthnight Ball for President Washington. He wrote to a friend about his experience.

Presidents' Day Celebrations

Several states celebrate both Washington's and Lincoln's birthdays on Presidents' Day. Some states refer to it as Washington-Lincoln Day or Lincoln-Washington Day. Many communities honor other presidents, too.

⭐ In 1971, President Richard Nixon declared a single national holiday in honor of all U.S. presidents.

Presidents' Day is a time to think about what it means to be American, and to appreciate the leadership shown by leaders of the United States in important periods of history.

In preparation for Presidents' Day, students learn about U.S. presidents. They read well-known presidential speeches and **biographies**. They may sing patriotic songs, perform plays, make crafts, or work on special projects. Most schools have their Presidents' Day activities on the last day of school before the holiday.

Independence Around the World

AUSTRALIA

The queen of Great Britain's birthday is celebrated in Australia on the second Monday in June. For many Australians, the Queen's Birthday is a time to visit with their family or go to a sporting event.

MEXICO

Each year on March 21, Mexicans celebrate the birth of Benito Juarez. Juarez was president of Mexico from 1861 to 1872. He is known as the "Mexican Lincoln." Fireworks and parties are held in his honor.

GREAT BRITAIN

The queen's birthday is celebrated on the first, second, or third Saturday in June. Many people gather with family and friends to celebrate. The queen attends a large parade by Great Britain's top soldiers.

Celebrating Today

On Presidents' Day, government offices and schools are closed. Some radio stations air special Presidents' Day broadcasts. Some television stations show movies about U.S. presidents. Newspapers sometimes print articles about presidents and local Presidents' Day events.

Activities and celebrations are held across the United States to honor U.S. presidents. Many businesses, such as restaurants and stores, offer special sales on the holiday. People attend banquets, parades, or wreath-laying ceremonies at historic sites across the United States on Presidents' Day.

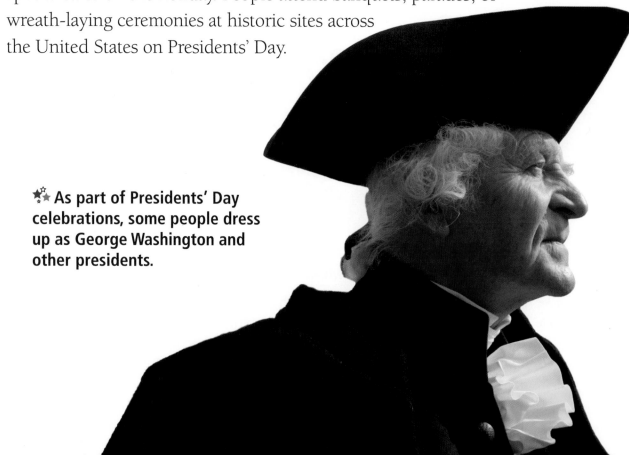

★★ As part of Presidents' Day celebrations, some people dress up as George Washington and other presidents.

Many Americans celebrate Presidents' Day by attending parades or other ceremonies. The patriotic colors of red, white, and blue are on display.

Presidents' Day in the United States

Activities and celebrations are held across the United States to honor U.S. presidents. This map shows a few examples.

KANSAS Every February, Lincoln, Kansas, celebrates Lincoln's birthday with a "reenactment weekend." Actors portray Abraham Lincoln and other people from the Civil War era. Participants enjoy patriotic music, buffalo stew, a president's ball, and a Lincoln look-alike contest.

Kansas

TEXAS Citizens of Laredo, Texas, hold one of the largest annual Presidents' Day celebrations in the country. They have celebrated the anniversary of Washington's birthday since 1898. The events last about two weeks. They include a ball, fireworks, music, and parades.

Texas

Hawai'i

Alaska

0   970 Miles

0   1,278 Miles

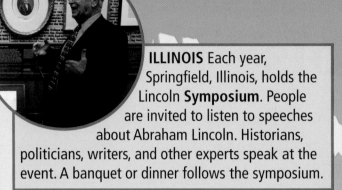

ILLINOIS Each year, Springfield, Illinois, holds the Lincoln **Symposium**. People are invited to listen to speeches about Abraham Lincoln. Historians, politicians, writers, and other experts speak at the event. A banquet or dinner follows the symposium.

WASHINGTON, D.C. The Washington Monument, a white marble structure, stands more than 555 feet high. The Lincoln Memorial has 36 columns and houses a sculpture of Lincoln sitting in a chair. Both monuments are located in Washington, D.C. Presidents' Day events at these sites have included patriotic music, speeches, and wreath-laying ceremonies.

Illinois

Virginia

VIRGINIA The Birthnight Ball, a celebration in honor of Washington's birthday, was first held at Gadsby's Tavern in Alexandria, Virginia, in 1797. Today, it is an annual event featuring a banquet and traditional dances. Thousands of people also visit Washington's home at Mount Vernon on Presidents' Day for wreath-laying ceremonies and historic presentations at Washington's tomb.

N
W E
S

0   207 Miles

Presidents' Day Symbols

United States presidents are often featured on television shows and in newspaper articles. Citizens learn about U.S. presidents at school and on trips to historic sites. There are many presidential symbols that help people remember the efforts and achievements of presidents.

MOUNT RUSHMORE NATIONAL MEMORIAL

The faces of George Washington, Thomas Jefferson, Theodore Roosevelt, and Abraham Lincoln are carved into the side of Mount Rushmore. It took designer Gutzon Borglum and a team of 400 workers 14 years to complete. They used tools, such as drills and hammers, to create the 60-foot high faces.

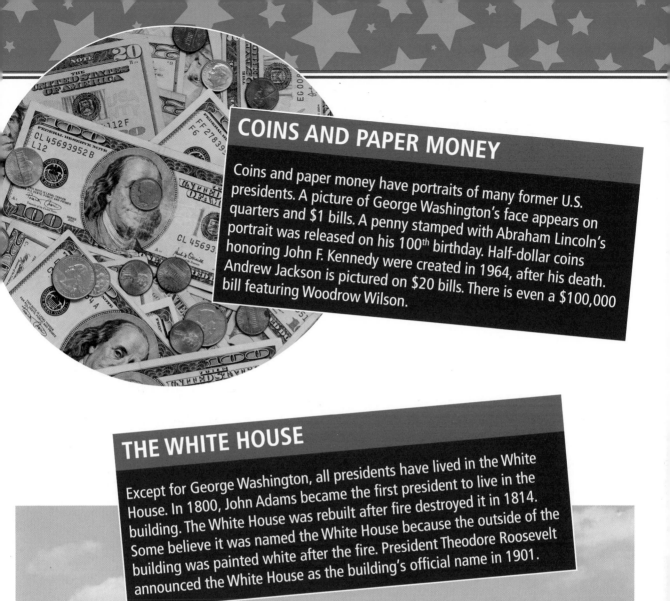

COINS AND PAPER MONEY

Coins and paper money have portraits of many former U.S. presidents. A picture of George Washington's face appears on quarters and $1 bills. A penny stamped with Abraham Lincoln's portrait was released on his 100th birthday. Half-dollar coins honoring John F. Kennedy were created in 1964, after his death. Andrew Jackson is pictured on $20 bills. There is even a $100,000 bill featuring Woodrow Wilson.

THE WHITE HOUSE

Except for George Washington, all presidents have lived in the White House. In 1800, John Adams became the first president to live in the building. The White House was rebuilt after fire destroyed it in 1814. Some believe it was named the White House because the outside of the building was painted white after the fire. President Theodore Roosevelt announced the White House as the building's official name in 1901.

A Speech to Remember

On November 19, 1863, President Abraham Lincoln presented the Gettysburg Address at the Gettysburg National Cemetery. The speech honored the soldiers who died fighting in the Civil War. This is a sample from the Gettysburg Address.

"It is rather for us to be here dedicated to the great task remaining before us - that from these honored dead we take increased devotion to that cause for which they gave the last full measure of devotion - that we here highly resolve that these dead shall not have died in vain - that this nation, under God, shall have a new birth of freedom - and that government of the people, by the people, for the people, shall not perish from the earth."

Abraham Lincoln

Write Your Own Speech

The president gives many important speeches throughout the year. These speeches may include plans for the future of the nation or words of encouragement. Imagine you are the president and you must give a speech to the nation. Try writing about a topic that is important to you and your friends.

Think about the people who will be listening to your speech. What are their ages, cultural backgrounds, interests, and careers? Choose a topic that will be of interest to this group of people.

Think of a person or cause that you would like to support or something you would like to change to improve the world.

Brainstorm ideas for your speech. Write a concept web outlining some of things you would like to say. Then, write your ideas as complete sentences. Be sure to use language that will entice your audience to listen.

Lincoln Pendant

There are many fun crafts you can make for Presidents' Day. For example, you can use a penny to make a President Abraham Lincoln pendant.

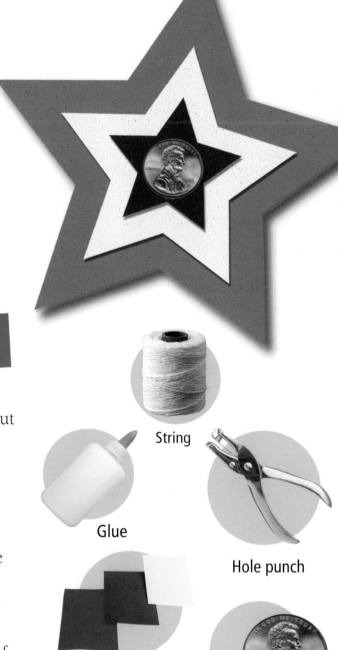

4 Easy Steps to Complete Your Pendant

1 To begin, cut a 4-inch star out of red craft paper.

2 Next, cut a 3-inch star out of white craft paper, and a 2-inch star out of blue craft paper.

3 Glue the stars together. Glue a penny in the center of the blue star. Make sure you can see Lincoln's face.

4 Punch a hole near the top of the red star, and thread a string through the star. Wear the pendant around your neck to celebrate Presidents' Day.

String

Glue

Hole punch

Red, white, and blue craft paper

One penny

Cherry Thumbprint Cookies

Ingredients

1 teaspoon vanilla
2 sticks butter or margarine
2 egg yolks
1/2 cup brown sugar

2 cups flour
1/2 teaspoon salt
maraschino cherries

Equipment

large bowl
wooden spoon

cookie sheet

Directions

Ask an adult for help with this recipe.

1. Preheat oven to 350 degrees Fahrenheit.
2. Put the vanilla, butter, egg yolks, and brown sugar in the large bowl. Blend together until creamy using the wooden spoon.
3. Add the flour and salt to the mixture, and blend well.
4. Roll the dough into 1-inch balls. Place each ball on a greased cookie sheet.
5. Make a thumbprint in each ball, and place a maraschino cherry in each thumbprint.
6. Bake the cookies for 8 to 10 minutes.

Test Your Knowledge!

1

What document did Abraham Lincoln issue that brought an end to slavery?

2

What are the names of the presidents carved into Mount Rushmore?

3

Which president was the first to have a national holiday in honor of his birthday?

4

What are some other names for Presidents' Day?

5
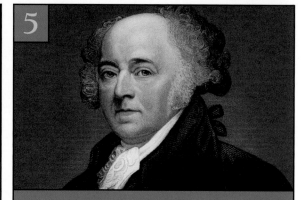

Who was the first president to live in the White House?

Quiz Answers:

1. Abraham Lincoln issued the Emancipation Proclamation in 1863. This led to the end of slavery.
2. The faces of Thomas Jefferson, Abraham Lincoln, Theodore Roosevelt, and George Washington are carved in the side of Mount Rushmore.
3. George Washington was the first president to have his birthday celebrated as a national holiday.
4. Some states still call Presidents' Day Washington's Birthday. Others refer to Presidents' Day as Washington-Lincoln Day or Lincoln-Washington Day.
5. John Adams was the first president to live in the White House.

Glossary

American Revolution: the war from 1775 to 1783 between the United States and Great Britain over American independence

ball: a fancy dancing party

biographies: books that tell the story of a person's life

Civil War: the war fought in the United States between the North and the South, from 1861 to 1865

colonists: people who live in a country that is ruled by another country

Emancipation Proclamation: Lincoln's announcement in 1863 that slaves were free

monarch: a nation's ruler or head of state

patriotic: showing love for one's country

slavery: when one person owns another person

symposium: a gathering during which people discuss a topic of interest

Index

Log on to www.av2books.com

AV² by Weigl brings you media enhanced books that support active learning. Go to **www.av2books.com**, and enter the special code inside the front cover of this book. You will gain access to enriched and enhanced content that supplements and complements this book. Content includes video, audio, web links, quizzes, a slide show, and activities.

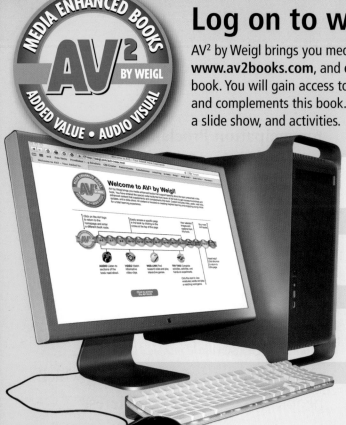

Audio
Listen to sections of the book read aloud.

Video
Watch informative video clips.

Web Link
Find research sites and play interactive games.

Try This!
Complete activities and hands-on experiments.

WHAT'S ONLINE?

 Try This!
Complete activities and hands-on experiments.

 Web Link
Find research sites and play interactive games.

Video
Watch informative video clips.

EXTRA FEATURES

Pages 8-9 Write a biography about an important person

Pages 10-11 Describe the features and special events of a similar celebration around the world

Pages 14-15 Complete a mapping activity about Presidents' Day celebrations

Pages 16-17 Try this activity about important holiday symbols

Pages 20-21 Play an interactive activity

Pages 6-7 Find out more about the history of Presidents' Day

Pages 10-11 Learn more about similar celebrations around the world

Pages 16-17 Find information about important holiday symbols

Pages 18-19 Link to more information about Presidents' Day

Pages 20-21 Check out more holiday craft ideas

Pages 4-5 Watch a video about Presidents' Day

Pages 12-13 Check out a video about how people celebrate Presidents' Day

 Audio
Hear introductory audio at the top of every page

Key Words
Study vocabulary, and play a matching word game.

Slide Show
View images and captions, and try a writing activity.

AV² Quiz
Take this quiz to test your knowledge

Due to the dynamic nature of the Internet, some of the URLs and activities provided as part of AV² by Weigl may have changed or ceased to exist. AV² by Weigl accepts no responsibility for any such changes. All media enhanced books are regularly monitored to update addresses and sites in a timely manner. Contact AV² by Weigl at 1-866-649-3445 or av2books@weigl.com with any questions, comments, or feedback.